D1144352

W Drawn

0477796309

About the authors

Steve Biddle is a professional entertainer and Origami expert. He has been teaching Origami to children and adults since 1976. While he was in Japan studying under the top Japanese Origami Masters, he met and married his wife Megumi. Megumi is one of the foremost Japanese paper artists working in *Washi* hand-made Japanese paper, and her work has received many top awards in Japan and abroad. She has designed for some of Japan's top fashion designers, and has worked on many award-winning commercials for Japanese television. Since their return to England, Steve and Megumi have taken their craft all over the country to schools, festivals and arts centres, and have designed for television and feature films. They present Origami as entertainment, art and education to young and old alike.

WEST LANCASHIRE
DISTRICT LIBRARIES

W/K	W/B
W/O	W/A
W/U	W/T
W/M	W/R
W/N	W/P 6/91

*Also available in Red Fox
by Steve and Megumi Biddle*

**Things to Make in the Holidays
Newspaper Magic
The Paint and Print Fun Book
Magical String
Amazing Origami**

AMAZING FLYING OBJECTS

Steve and Megumi Biddle

Illustrations by Megumi Biddle

RED FOX

A Red Fox Book
Published by Arrow Books Limited
20 Vauxhall Bridge Road, London SW1V 2SA

An imprint of the Random Century Group

London Melbourne Sydney Auckland
Johannesburg and agencies throughout the world

Red Fox edition 1991

Text © Steve and Megumi Biddle 1991
Illustrations © Megumi Biddle 1991

The right of Steve and Megumi Biddle to be identified
as the authors and illustrator of this work has been
asserted by them, in accordance with the Copyright,
Designs and Patents Act, 1988.

047796309

This book is sold subject to the condition that it shall
not, by way of trade or otherwise, be lent, resold, hired
out, or otherwise circulated without the publisher's
prior consent in any form of binding or cover other than
that in which it is published and without a similar condition including this condition being imposed on the sub-
sequent purchaser.

Set in Times
by JH Graphics Ltd, Reading

Made and printed in Great Britain by
The Guernsey Press Co Ltd
Guernsey. C.I.

ISBN 0 09 964480 0

Contents

Introduction

AMAZING FLYING OBJECTS is full of ideas that you can make by yourself and also enjoy with your friends. Every item begins with a short list of materials that you need to get you started. More often than not all that you require is a pencil, ruler, scissors, paper and a few other everyday materials that can be easily found around the home.

When you are throwing any flying object always be very careful NOT to hit anyone (especially in their eyes). Also never throw any flying object where it could do damage to property, like your parents' best dinner service.

When you try the models in this book use your imagination and experiment to see what new types of flying objects you can create. As no two flying objects ever fly the same, do not be disheartened if yours does not fly well first time around. Make sure that it is not bent out of shape or wrinkled in any way. If nothing works, just place your flying object to one side and make another one.

We would very much like to hear from you concerning your interest in flying objects. So please write to us, care of the publishers, enclosing a stamped, addressed envelope.

We hope that you have a great deal of fun and enjoyment with AMAZING FLYING OBJECTS!

Steve and Megumi

Acknowledgements

We would like to thank Mitsuhiro Matsumoto and Toshie Takahama for sharing their knowledge of paper aeroplanes with us. Also Tomomi Kimura for showing us many of the other amazing flying objects.

Flying Fish

This is a very easy flying object to make. It will twist and turn around.

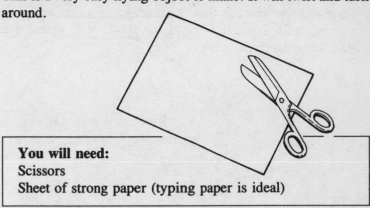

You will need:
Scissors
Sheet of strong paper (typing paper is ideal)

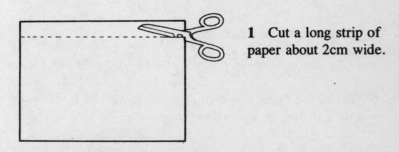

1 Cut a long strip of paper about 2cm wide.

2 Turn the strip around so that it is sideways on. On the lower right-hand side, cut a slit half way across the strip. Repeat on the upper left-hand side.

3 Bring the right-hand slit over to meet the left-hand slit and . . .

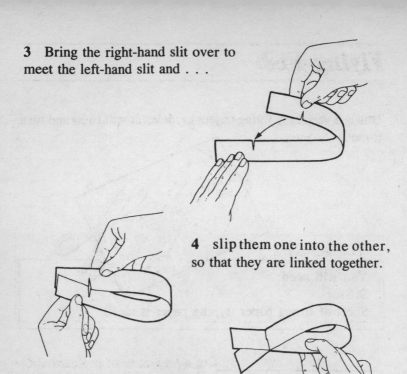

4 slip them one into the other, so that they are linked together.

5 This is what your completed flying fish should look like.

6 Throw the flying fish high up into the air and it will twist and turn around on its way to the ground.

Helicopter

This is a fun flying object to make. It will turn around just like a real helicopter.

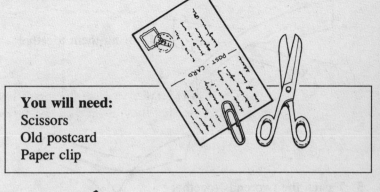

> **You will need:**
> Scissors
> Old postcard
> Paper clip

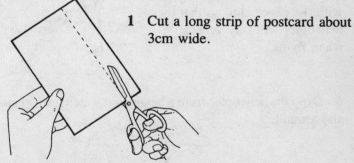

1 Cut a long strip of postcard about 3cm wide.

2 Turn the strip around so that it is sideways on. Make two slits in the strip as shown, being careful each time to cut only two-thirds of the distance.

3 Hold the upper right-hand end and the lower left-hand end and . . .

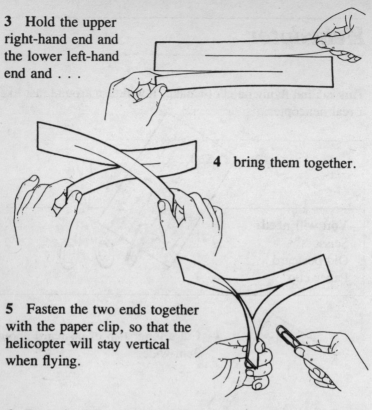

4 bring them together.

5 Fasten the two ends together with the paper clip, so that the helicopter will stay vertical when flying.

6 Drop the helicopter from a height and watch it whirl around and around.

Twister

Around and around and down . . . this flying object will glide with its wings twisting around.

> **You will need:**
> Scissors
> Old postcard
> Paper clip

1 Cut a long strip of postcard about 1cm wide.

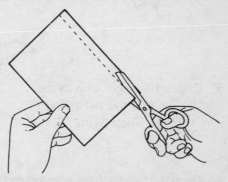

2 Turn the strip around so that it is lengthways on. Fold the bottom end of the strip up, so making a V-like shape.

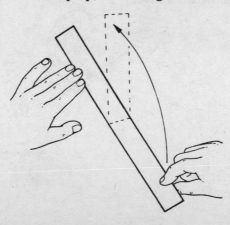

3 Fold the right-hand end forwards and the left-hand end backwards.

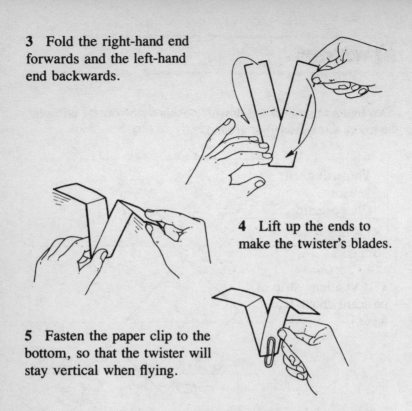

4 Lift up the ends to make the twister's blades.

5 Fasten the paper clip to the bottom, so that the twister will stay vertical when flying.

6 Drop the twister from a height and watch it twist around and around. You can make it go faster or slower by varying the length of the twister's blades.

Spinner

This flying object comes from Japan. Make many of them, in different sizes, and drop them gently to see them fly.

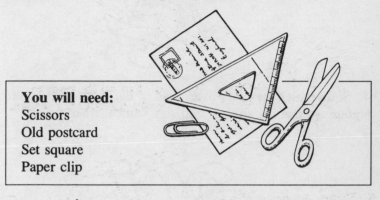

You will need:
Scissors
Old postcard
Set square
Paper clip

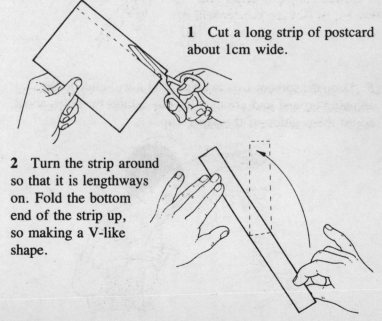

1 Cut a long strip of postcard about 1cm wide.

2 Turn the strip around so that it is lengthways on. Fold the bottom end of the strip up, so making a V-like shape.

3 With the set square gently curl both the ends.

4 Softly bend the ends over. Fasten the paper clip to the bottom, so that the spinner will stay vertical when flying.

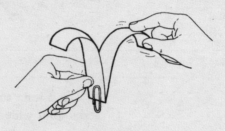

5 Drop the spinner from a height and it will glide to the floor spinning around and around. If your spinner wobbles about, adjust the position of the paper clip.

Flying Knot

One day, while we were playing about with a strip of paper, we invented this flying object quite by accident.

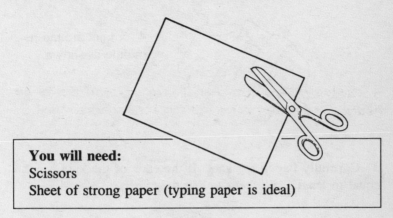

You will need:
Scissors
Sheet of strong paper (typing paper is ideal)

1 Cut a long strip of paper about 3cm wide.

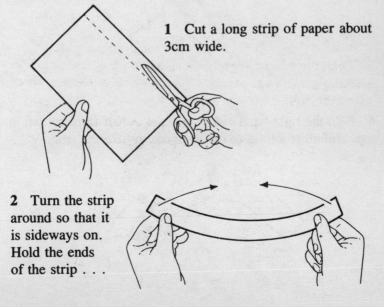

2 Turn the strip around so that it is sideways on. Hold the ends of the strip . . .

3 and tie . . .

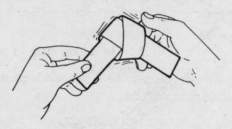

4 a knot around its middle as shown.

5 Carefully flatten the knot. If the ends of the knot are not equal in length, cut them so that they are.

6 Fold the right-hand end of the knot in half from bottom to top. Unfold it a little so that it stands up like the letter V.

7 Turn the knot over from side to side and repeat step 6.

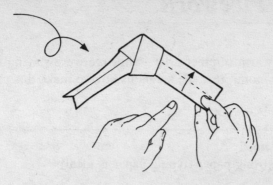

8 Hold the knot between the forefinger and thumb . . .

9 and drop it from a height. The knot will float down, going around and around in a spiral.

Paper Firework

It was on a warm summer's day, while we were staying with our niece Tomomi, that she taught us how to make this paper firework.

You will need:
Sheet of strong paper (typing paper is ideal)
Scissors
Cardboard tube (the inside of a kitchen paper roll is ideal)
Pencil
Sticky tape
Stapler

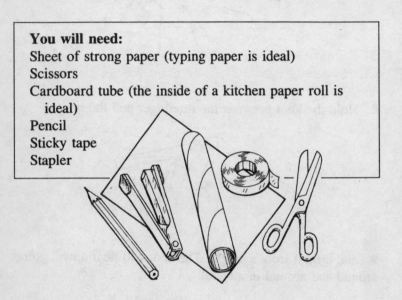

1 Place the sheet of paper on a flat surface, sideways on. Fold and unfold it in half from bottom to top.

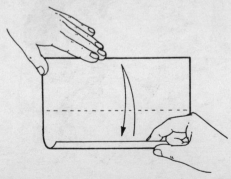

2 Cut the paper in half along the fold-line. Place the top half to one side.

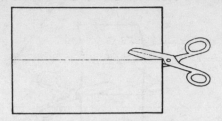

3 Turn the bottom half of the paper so that it is lengthways on. Place the cardboard tube on to the paper's top edge.

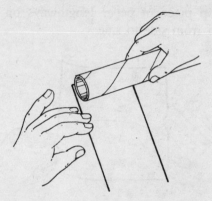

4 Roll the paper around the cardboard tube. Draw a pencil line along the edge where the paper overlaps.

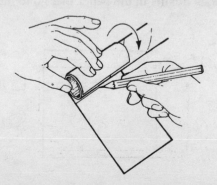

5 Cut along the pencil line and place the bottom piece of paper to one side.

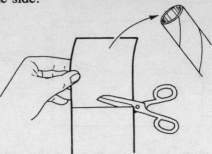

6 Place the top piece of paper lengthways on. Fold and unfold it in half from side to side.

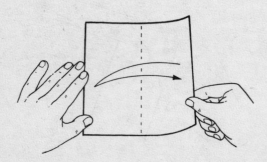

7 Turn the paper over from side to side. From the right-hand side cut a series of slits in the paper that go to meet the middle fold-line.

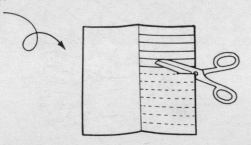

8 Roll the paper up into a tube that is slightly smaller in diameter than the cardboard tube.

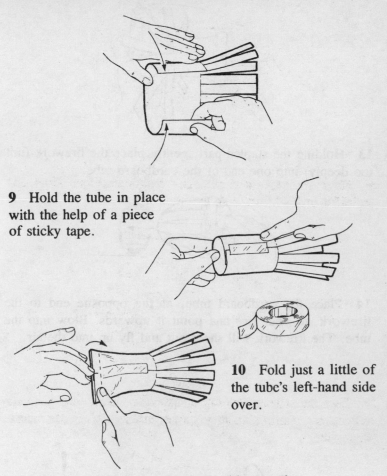

9 Hold the tube in place with the help of a piece of sticky tape.

10 Fold just a little of the tube's left-hand side over.

11 Hold the folded part in place with a staple.

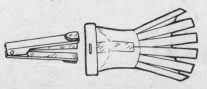

12 Carefully bend the strips over the stapled part, so making the paper firework.

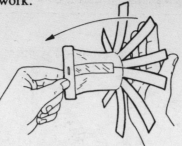

13 Holding the stapled part, gently place the firework (not too deeply) into one end of the cardboard tube.

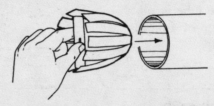

14 Place the cardboard tube, at the opposite end to the firework, to your lips and point it upwards. Blow into the tube. The firework will shoot out and fly up into the air.

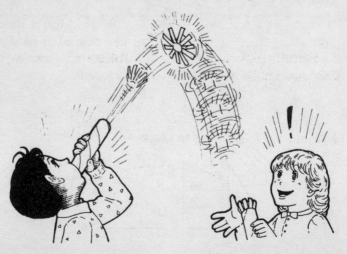

The Circular Airfoil

The circular airfoil is a fun thing to fly, once you get the hang of it.

You will need:
Sheet of strong paper (typing paper is ideal)
Scissors
Sticky tape

1 Place the sheet of paper on a flat surface, sideways on. Fold and unfold it in half from side to side.

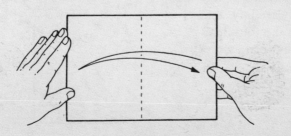

2 From the right-hand side make three slits in the paper as shown, being careful each time to cut only a quarter of the distance to the middle fold-line.

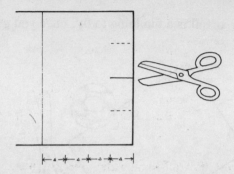

3 Once again from the right-hand side make four slits in the paper as shown, being careful each time to cut only a quarter of the distance to the middle fold-line. You have now made the circular airfoil's fins.

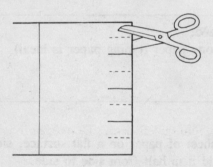

4 Fold each of the fins over. Carefully note where the fold-lines start and end.

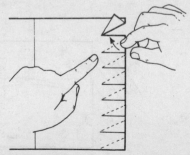

5 Fold the left-hand side over to meet the middle fold-line.

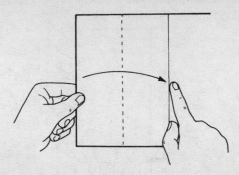

6 Again fold the left-hand side over to meet the middle fold-line.

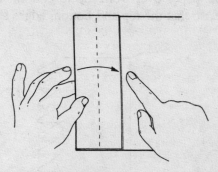

7 Once again fold the left-hand side over to meet the middle fold-line.

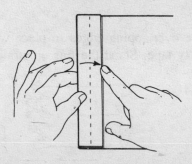

8 Last of all fold the left-hand side over along the middle fold-line. Press the paper flat.

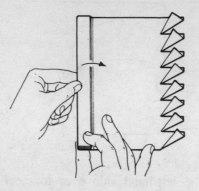

9 Turn the paper over from top to bottom. Bend the paper into a tube, so that the top and bottom edges slightly overlap.

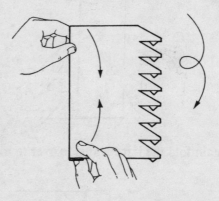

10 Hold the overlapping edges in place with the help of a piece of sticky tape. Stand the fins up straight.

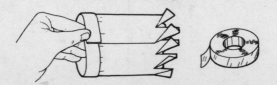

11 Hold the circular airfoil near its fins . . .

12 and throw it over-arm. The circular airfoil will glide through the air, spinning around as it goes.

Jumping Bug

One of our friends showed us how to make this noisy jumping bug when we were teaching origami at our local library.

You will need:
Two 10cm squares of strong paper (typing paper is ideal)
Glue
Medium-sized elastic band

---

1 Tightly roll each piece of paper into a firm cylinder.

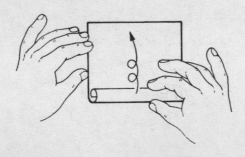

2 Hold each cylinder in place with the help of a little glue.

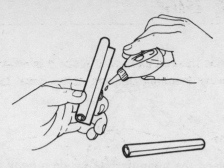

3 When the glue is dry bend each cylinder in the middle.

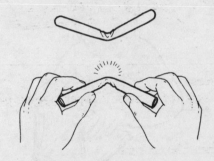

4 Twist the elastic band several times around the middle of the cylinders.

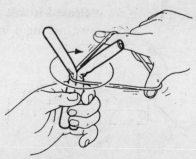

5 Hold one cylinder still and wind the other as tightly as possible.

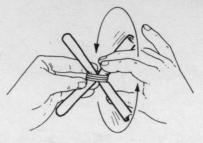

6 Carefully place the jumping bug inside a book.

7 When the jumping bug is released it will fly up into the air, making a loud rattling noise.

Butterfly

We are sure that you will have a lot of fun with this flying object. The secret to it is in the elastic band.

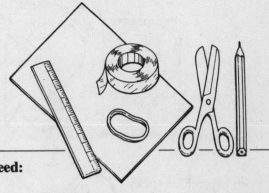

You will need:
Scissors
Piece of strong cardboard (the back of a note pad is
    ideal)
Ruler
Pencil
Sticky tape
Medium-sized elastic band

1 Cut two cardboard rectangles, both measuring 5cm × 7cm.

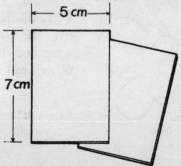

2 Turn one rectangle around so that it is lengthways on. Using the pencil, copy this design on to it. Carefully cut around your pencil lines and discard the shaded parts. Repeat this step with the remaining rectangle.

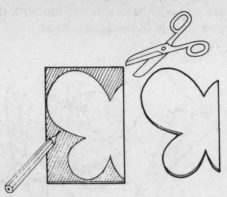

3 With a piece of sticky tape fasten together the two designs, to make the shape of a butterfly.

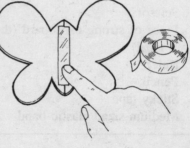

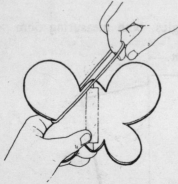

4 Loop the elastic band over the butterfly's left-hand wing and the right-hand side of its head.

5 Twist the elastic band and loop it over the butterfly's right-hand wing.

6 Once again twist the elastic band and . . .

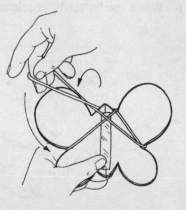

7 loop it back over the butterfly's right-hand wing and the left-hand side of its head.

8 For the last time, twist the elastic band and loop it back over the butterfly's left-hand wing.

9 This should be your finished result.

10 Keeping the butterfly flat, carefully place it inside a book.

11 When the butterfly is released, it will fly up into the air.

Jumping Frog

This is a very simple flying object to make. It has a great action mechanism.

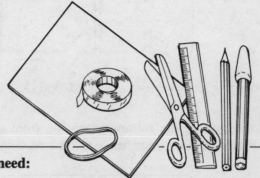

You will need:
Scissors
Piece of strong cardboard (the back of a note pad is
    ideal)
Ruler
Pencil
Sticky tape
Medium-sized elastic band
Felt-tip pen

1   Cut two cardboard rectangles, both measuring 6cm × 8cm.

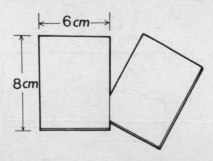

2 Leaving a space of about 2mm between each rectangle place them sideways on.

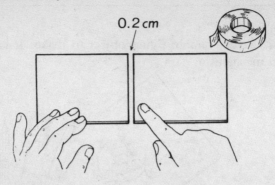

3 Join together the rectangles on the front and back with sticky tape. Cut two notches into each rectangle as shown.

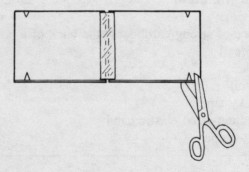

4 Loop the elastic band over the notches on the left-hand side.

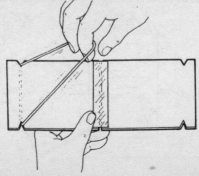

5 Twist the elastic band and, being careful to keep the rectangles flat, loop it over the notches on the right-hand side.

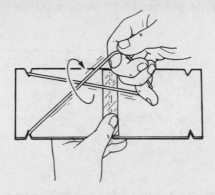

6 This should be your finished result.

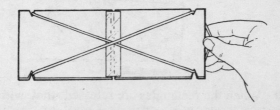

7 Gently let the elastic band pull the rectangles together. With the felt-tip pen draw a picture of a frog on to the top rectangle.

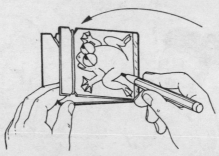

8 Carefully open out the rectangles back to step 6. Fold them in half away from you, so that you stretch the elastic band and at the same time put the frog's picture on the inside.

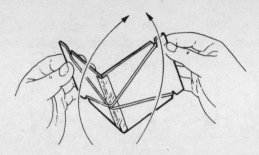

9 Keeping the rectangles folded in half, place them on a flat surface.

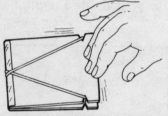

10 When the rectangles are released, they will jump up into the air and the frog will appear with a loud snap.

Shooting Rocket

Five, four, three, two, one . . . we have lift off! This rocket may not get you to the Moon but you will have fun making it.

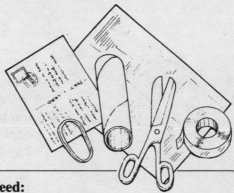

You will need:
Scissors
Cardboard tube (the inside of a kitchen paper roll is ideal)
Medium-sized elastic band
Sticky tape
Page of newspaper
Old postcard

1 In one end of the cardboard tube cut two small flaps that are opposite to each other.

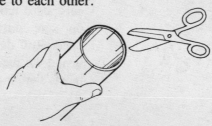

2 Fold the flaps outwards and loop the elastic band over them.

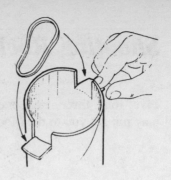

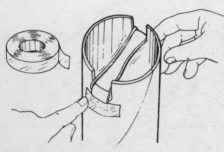

3 Fold the flaps down and fasten them on to the cardboard tube with pieces of sticky tape.

4 Crush the page of newspaper into a small ball. Wrap sticky tape all around the ball to make it firm and tight, so that it can loosely fit inside the cardboard tube.

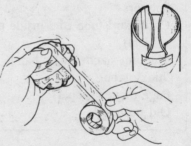

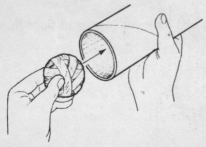

5 Place the ball into the cardboard tube, at the opposite end to the elastic band. Roll the ball down inside the tube until it meets the elastic band.

6 Firmly fasten together the ball and elastic band with a piece of sticky tape.

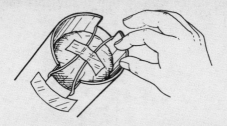

7 Place the old postcard on a flat surface, lengthways on. Roll it into a tube that is . . .

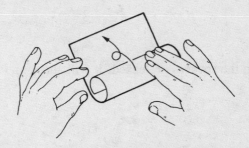

8 slightly smaller in diameter than the cardboard tube. Hold the tube in place with the help of a piece of sticky tape, so making the rocket. Place the rocket on to the elastic band.

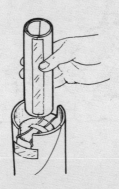

9 With the rocket pointing UPWARDS, place the cardboard tube on a flat surface. Push the rocket down inside the cardboard tube, far enough so that it stretches the elastic band.

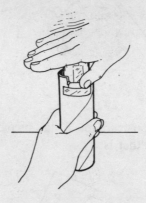

10 When the rocket is released, it will shoot up into the air.

Super Rocket

If the previous rocket could not get you to the Moon, maybe this one will take you there instead.

> **You will need:**
> Compasses
> Sheet of strong paper (typing paper is ideal)
> Pencil
> Scissors
> Glue
> Ruler
> Empty washing-up liquid bottle

1 Using the compasses, mark and measure out the semicircle on to the sheet of paper, as shown. Carefully cut around your pencil line. Do not discard any excess paper.

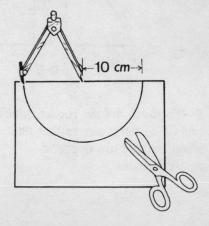

←10 cm→

2 Bend the semicircle so that its sides slightly overlap.

3 Glue the overlapping sides together, to make a cone.

4 Using the pencil and ruler, mark and measure out the rocket's fins on the excess paper, as shown. Carefully cut around your pencil lines.

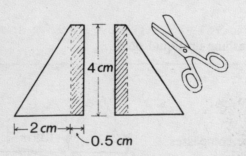

4 cm

|←—2 cm—→| 0.5 cm

5 To finish off the rocket, glue the fins on to the cone, so that they stand out and are opposite to each other.

6 Remove the washing-up liquid bottle's cap. Place the rocket over the bottle's nozzle.

7 With the rocket pointing UPWARDS, place the bottle on a flat surface. Firmly press together the bottle's sides so that you force . . .

8 the air inside to rush out and fire the rocket up into the air.

Rocket and Launching Pad

Perhaps with this rocket and launching pad you can explore deep into outer space?

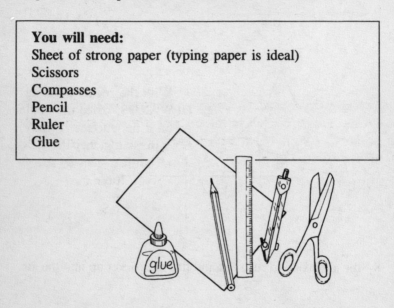

You will need:
Sheet of strong paper (typing paper is ideal)
Scissors
Compasses
Pencil
Ruler
Glue

1 Place the sheet of paper on a flat surface, sideways on. Fold the left-hand side over to lie along the bottom edge, so that you make a triangle.

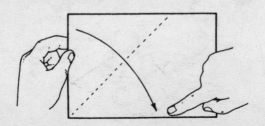

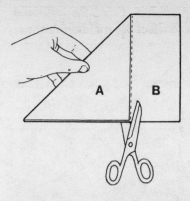

2 Cut along the right-hand edge of the triangle, so that you make triangle A and rectangle B.

3 Using the compasses, pencil and ruler, mark and measure out the quarter circle and the rocket's fins on to rectangle B, as shown. Carefully cut around your pencil lines and discard the shaded part.

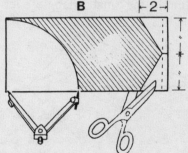

4 With the quarter circle repeat steps 2 and 3 of SUPER ROCKET (see page 45). To finish off the rocket, glue the fins on to the cone, so that they stand out and are opposite to each other.

5 Open out triangle A into a diamond. From the left-hand point fold the sloping edges over to meet the middle fold-line.

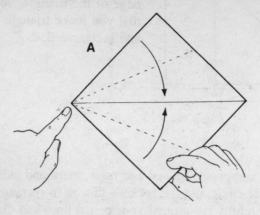

6 Fold and unfold the small triangle over the base of the larger one.

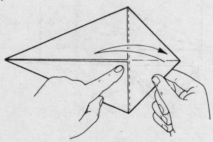

7 Along the fold-line made in step 6, tuck the small triangle up inside the larger one.

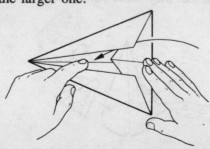

8 Once again from the left-hand point, fold the sloping edges over to meet the middle fold-line. Press the edges flat and unfold them.

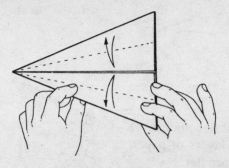

9 Fold the left-hand point over so that it overlaps the right-hand edge.

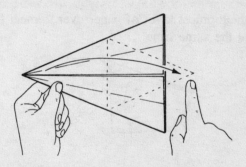

10 Fold the paper in half from bottom to top.

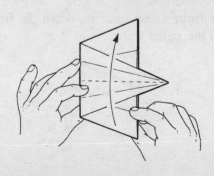

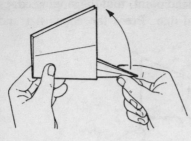

11 Holding the paper as shown, pull up the point that is sticking out, . . .

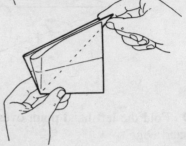

12 so that it becomes level with the top layers of paper. Press the paper flat.

13 Fold the topmost layer of paper over to meet the bottom edge and at the same time. . . ,

14 starting from its tip, narrow down the front part of the point. Press the paper flat.

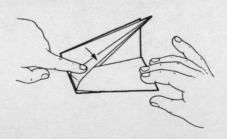

15 Turn the paper over from side to side and repeat steps 13 . . .

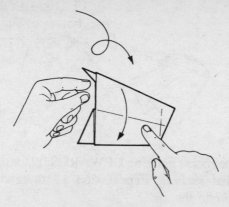

16 and 14, to make the launching pad.

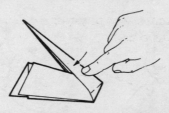

17 To work the launching pad, pull apart the bottom left-hand layers of paper, so that you make the point flick forwards.

18 Place the rocket on to the point.

19 With the rocket pointing UPWARDS, place the launching pad on a flat surface. Repeat step 17 to send the rocket shooting up into the air.

Unidentified Flying Object

One day, while we were watching a science fiction film, the idea of making this UFO came to us.

You will need:
Piece of card (an old cereal carton is ideal)
Pencil
Ruler
Scissors
Sticky tape

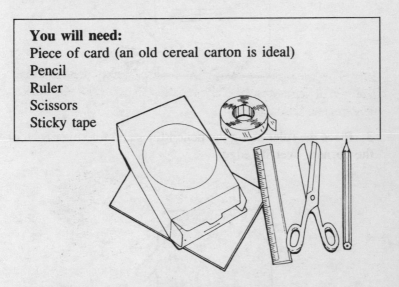

1 Using the pencil and ruler, mark and measure out the square and triangle as shown, on to the piece of card. Carefully cut around your pencil lines and discard the shaded part.

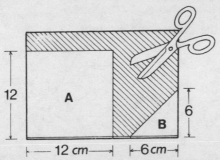

2 Using the pencil and ruler, mark and measure out the triangles, as shown, on to square A.

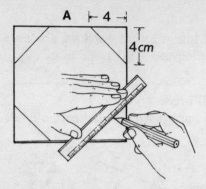

3 Place the ruler along the pencil lines and fold over each of the corners over its edge.

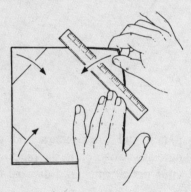

4 Stand the corners up straight.

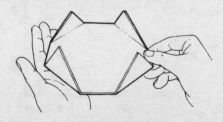

5 Turn square A over from side to side. Fasten triangle B on to the middle of square A with pieces of sticky tape.

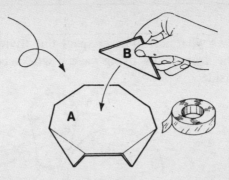

6 Grip one of square A's sides between the forefinger and middle finger. Release by . . .

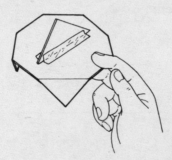

7 flicking your wrist forward. The UFO will spin into the air.

Flying Saucer

Who knows what part of outer space this flying object might have come from? The flying saucer works best when it is flown outside.

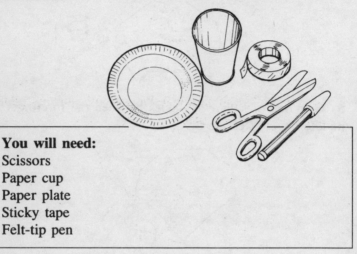

You will need:
Scissors
Paper cup
Paper plate
Sticky tape
Felt-tip pen

1 Cut the paper cup in half crossways, and discard the top part.

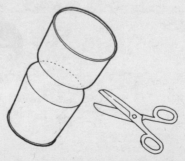

2 Cut slits along the top edge of the bottom part, so that you make a series of flaps. Bend the flaps outwards.

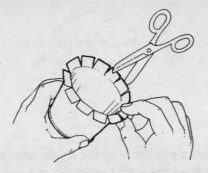

3 Fasten the bottom part on to the base of the paper plate by sticking the flaps with pieces of sticky tape.

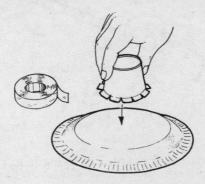

4 Cut eight slits around the rim of the plate, so that you make a series of flaps.

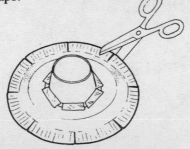

5 Fold each alternate flap either backwards or forwards.

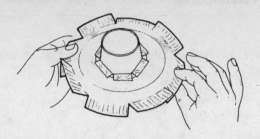

6 With the felt-tip pen draw on the flying saucer's windows. Grip one of the flaps between the thumb and fingers. Release by . . .

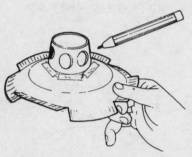

7 flicking your arm forward. The flying saucer will spin into the air.

Boomerang

Just like a real boomerang this one will fly back to you. Make sure that you have a lot of space to fly it in!

> **You will need:**
> Scissors
> Piece of card (an old cereal carton is ideal)
> Pencil
> Ruler
> Two-pence piece

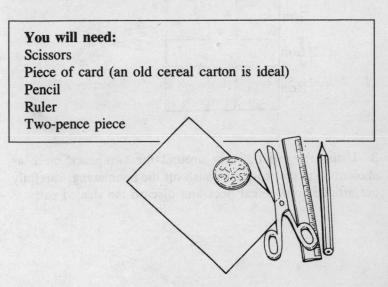

1 Cut a square of card measuring 8.5cm × 8.5cm.

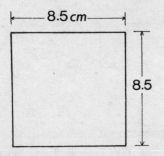

2 Using the pencil and ruler, mark and measure out the cross, as shown, on to the square. Carefully cut around your pencil lines and discard the shaded parts.

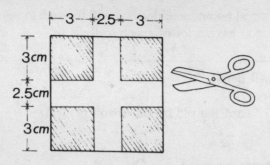

3 Using the pencil, mark around the two-pence piece as shown, on to the cross. To finish off the boomerang, carefully cut around your pencil lines and discard the shaded parts.

4 Place the boomerang on the back of your left hand so that one of its arms lies along your forefinger. Tuck your left thumb out of the way and with your right forefinger strike the edge of the arm which sticks out. The boomerang . . .

5 will spin away and return back to you.

Whirligig

We were shown how to make this flying object by a very good friend, Mitsuhiro Matsumoto, who lives in Hamamatsu, Japan.

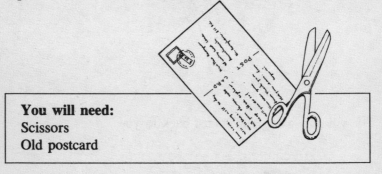

You will need:
Scissors
Old postcard

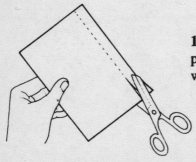

1 Cut three long strips of postcard each about 1.5cm wide.

2 Turn the strips around so that they are sideways on. Fold each strip A, B and C in half from right to left.

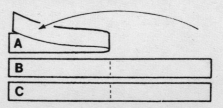

3 Take strips A and B and put A inside B like this.

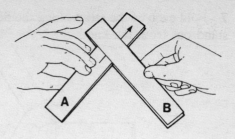

4 Weave strip C into place.

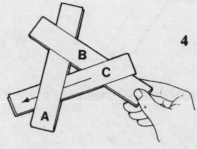

5 Pull the strips in the directions as shown . . .

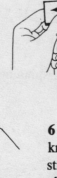

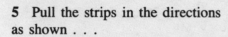

6 to make a tight paper knot. To help keep the strips tied together, crease along the dashed lines.

65

7 Fold each of the strips along the dashed lines, so that they stand out from the knot.

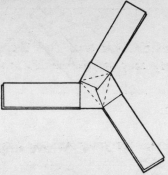

8 Repeat step 4 of the BOOMERANG (see page 61) . . .

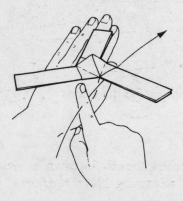

9 to send the whirligig spinning through the air.

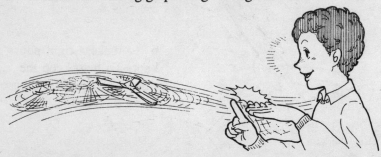

Frisbee

When we were on holiday in New York City, we came across this quick and very easy way to make a frisbee.

You will need:
Scissors
Five old envelopes (or you could use old postcards)
Ruler
Pencil
Sticky tape

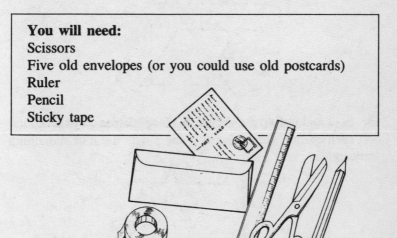

1 Making sure that the envelopes are sealed down, cut them into rectangles measuring 11cm × 15cm.

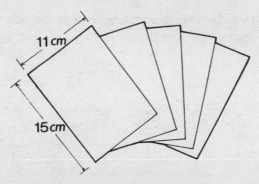

2 Turn one rectangle around so that it is lengthways on. Using the ruler and pencil draw a diagonal line from the top right-hand corner to the bottom left-hand corner.

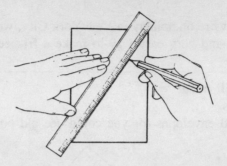

3 Fold and unfold the rectangle along the pencil line. Round off each corner. Repeat steps 2 and 3 with the four remaining rectangles.

4 As shown, lay the five rectangles side by side and with pieces of sticky tape join them together into a strip.

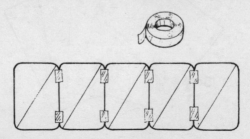

5 With the sticky tape on the outside, bend the strip around into a five-sided tube. Hold the tube together with two pieces of sticky tape.

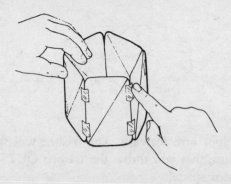

6 Push the tube down from the top and twist it along the pencil lines in an anticlockwise direction. (You may find this difficult first time around - do not give up hope.) Continue twisting . . .

7 and the tube will suddenly collapse into the shape of a frisbee.

8 To prevent the frisbee from coming apart, fasten together its sides with pieces of sticky tape. Grip one of the frisbee's sides between the thumb and fingers. Release by . . .

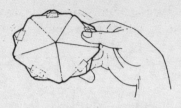

9 flicking your arm forward. The frisbee will spin into the air. Make sure that you throw the frisbee OUTSIDE where there is lots of space!

Loop Glider

Why not make several loop gliders and have long-distance gliding competitions with your friends?

> **You will need:**
> Scissors
> Sheet of strong paper (typing paper is ideal)
> Ruler
> Pencil
> Drinking straw
> Sticky tape

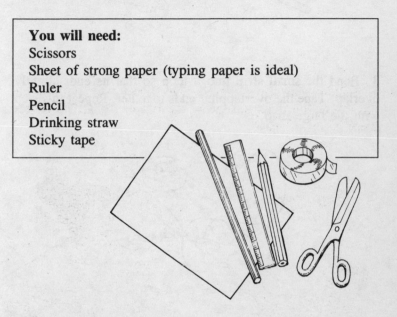

1 Cut two strips of paper, one measuring 2cm × 16cm and the other 2cm × 10cm.

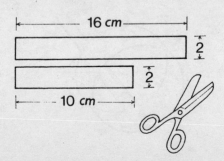

2 Cut the drinking straw so that it is 15cm long.

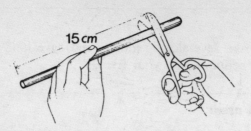

3 Bend the small strip into a loop so that its ends slightly overlap. Tape the overlapping ends together. Repeat this step with the large strip.

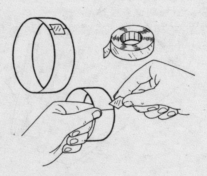

4 With a piece of sticky tape attach the small loop to one end of the drinking straw, and . . .

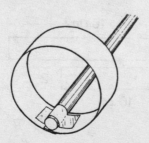

5 attach the large loop to the opposite end.

6 To fly the loop glider, hold it high with the small loop at the front and throw gently. The loop glider will glide through the air, losing height slowly. If the loop glider wobbles about adjust the position of the loops. See what happens when you fly the loop glider with the large loop at the front.

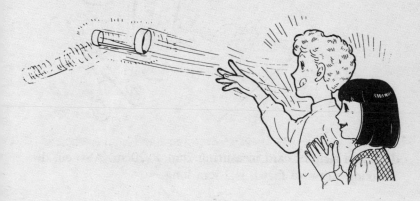

Dragonfly

This flying object comes from Japan, where it is called taketonbo (bamboo dragonfly). Not only does the dragonfly glide, it also climbs and hovers.

You will need:
Scissors
Piece of card (an old cereal carton is ideal)
Ruler
Pencil
Drinking straw
Sticky tape

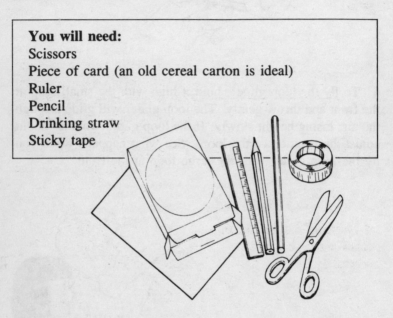

1 Cut a strip of card measuring 2cm × 20cm. Also cut the drinking straw so that it is 15cm long.

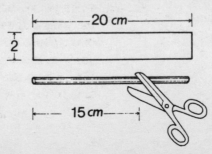

2 Using the ruler and pencil, mark and measure out the strip of card as shown. With the scissors, carefully cut a small cross in the middle of the strip.

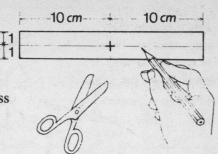

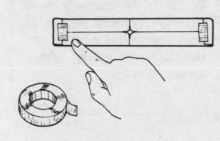

3 Fold over about 1cm of either end of the strip. Fasten these ends down with pieces of sticky tape. These are the dragonfly's wings. Turn the wings over from top to bottom.

4 Around one end of the straw wrap sticky tape so that . . .

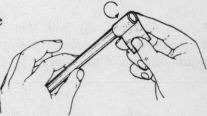

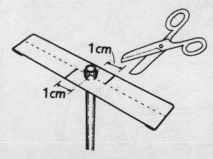

5 the taped end is a tight fit when placed into the cross in the wings. If the wings move about a little, tape the straw to the wings to hold it firm. Cut a slit on either side of the straw as shown.

6 From the slits outward, fold the wings down a little. Be careful to fold the wings down the same amount.

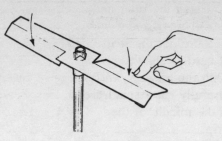

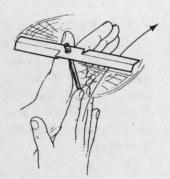

7 To fly the dragonfly, hold the straw between your palms. Roll your palms together so that the wings quickly turn around. Let go . . .

8 and the dragonfly will spin out of your hands. If the dragonfly does not climb or stops spinning straight away, adjust the fold in the wings.

Falling Leaf

One autumn day, while we were watching the leaves fall from the oak tree in our garden, this idea came to us.

You will need:
Two 10cm squares of strong paper (typing paper is ideal)
Glue

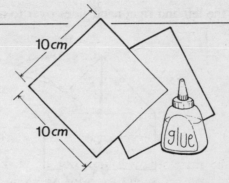

1 Place a square of paper on a flat surface. Fold and unfold it in half from side to side.

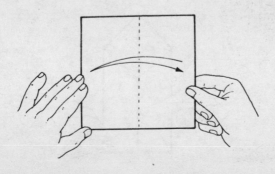

2 Fold the two top corners over to meet the middle fold-line.

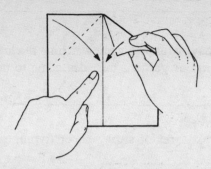

3 Fold the left and right-hand sides over to meet the middle fold-line.

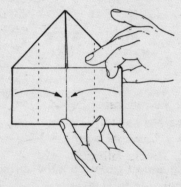

4 Fold the two bottom corners over to meet the middle fold-line.

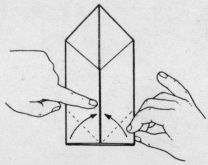

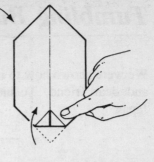

5 Turn the paper over. Fold the bottom point over a little. This is one half of the falling leaf.

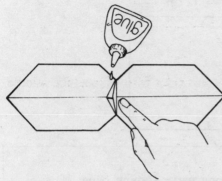

6 Repeat steps 1 to 5 with the remaining square of paper. Glue together both halves of the falling leaf at their bottom points.

7 To fly the falling leaf, hold the glued points and gently throw it forwards with a slight push. As the falling leaf flies forward . . .

8 it will twist over and over.

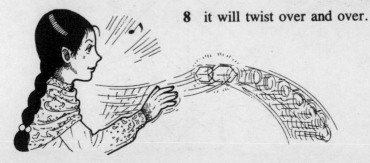

Tumbling Butterfly

We were shown how to make this flying object by a very kind and dear friend, Toshie Takahama, who lives in Tokyo, Japan.

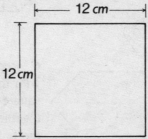

You will need:
A 12cm square of strong paper (typing paper is ideal)

1 Place the square of paper on a flat surface with a corner facing you so that it looks like a diamond. Fold it in half from right to left.

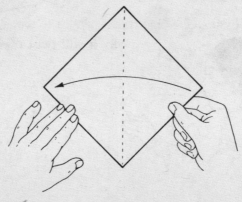

2 Fold and unfold it in half from bottom to top.

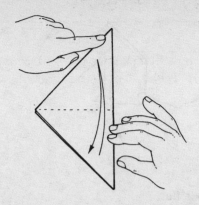

3 Fold the two left-hand points over so that they overlap the right-hand edge.

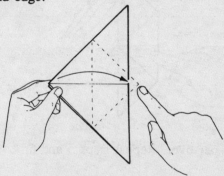

4 Fold the paper in half from bottom to top.

5 Fold the topmost flap down.

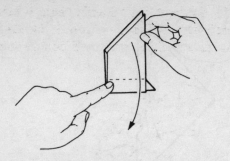

6 Press the paper flat.

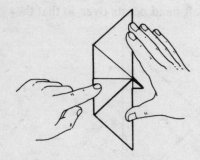

7 Turn the paper over. Repeat steps 5 and 6.

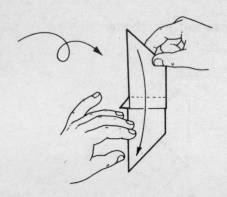

8 Lift the flaps up so that they are horizontal. Open out a little the two triangular pockets so finishing off the tumbling butterfly. To fly the tumbling butterfly, hold it between the thumb and forefinger and gently throw it forwards with a slight push. As the tumbling butterfly flies forwards . . .

9 it will tumble over and over.

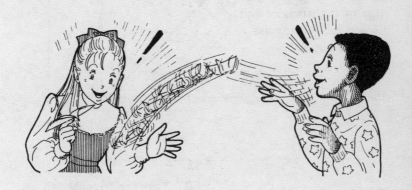

Sycamore Seed

We invented this flying object especially for this book. The sycamore seed may seem difficult at first but it is very easy to make.

You will need:
Sheet of thin but strong paper (airmail paper is ideal)
Scissors

---

1 Place the sheet of paper on a flat surface, sideways on. Fold the left-hand side over to lie along the top edge, so that you make a triangle. Cut along the right-hand side edge of the triangle, and discard the rectangular shape of paper.

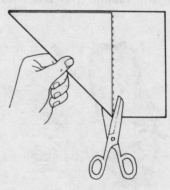

2 Turn the triangle around so that the tip faces upwards. Fold the triangle in half from right to left. Press the triangle flat.

3 Open the triangle out into a diamond.

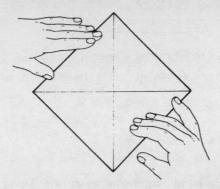

4 Fold the bottom and top corners into the middle.

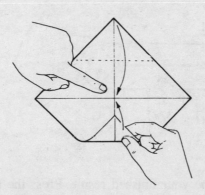

5 Fold the bottom and top edges over to meet the middle fold-line.

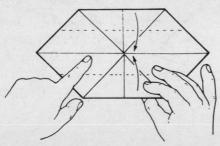

6 Fold the left-hand corner over as shown.

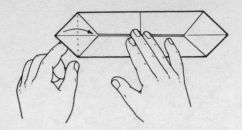

7 Fold the right-hand corner over as shown. This is the blade of the sycamore seed. Carefully note where the fold-line starts and ends.

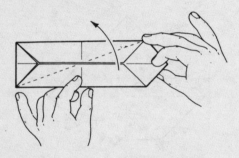

8 This should be your finished result. Press the paper flat.

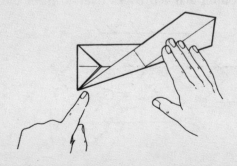

9 Fold the bottom left-hand corner up and at the same time slightly open the top layer of paper, so that . . .

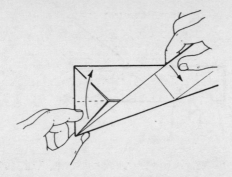

10 the middle stands up like a mountain.

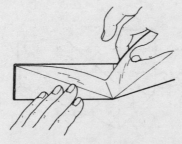

11 Press the mountain flat, rearranging the paper as shown.

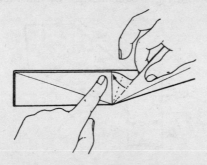

12 Start to make the sycamore seed's pod by folding the bottom left-hand edge over to lie along the middle.

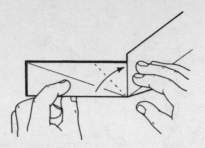

13 Fold the top left-hand flap behind by wrapping it over the top edge of the pod.

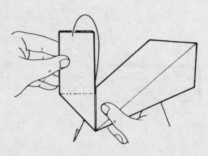

14 Fold the bottom right-hand corner of the flap over.

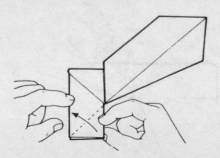

15 Fold the end of the flap over the sloping edge of the pod.

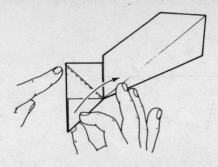

16 Tuck the tip of the flap into . . .

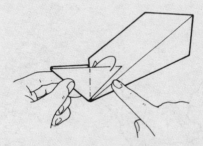

17 the pocket that is underneath. Press the paper flat, to finish off the sycamore seed.

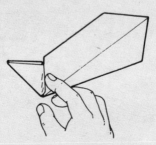

18   To fly the sycamore seed, hold its pod between the thumb and forefinger . . .

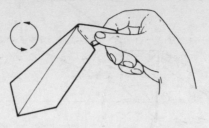

19   and throw it up into the air. The sycamore seed will fall to the ground with a gentle, spinning motion.

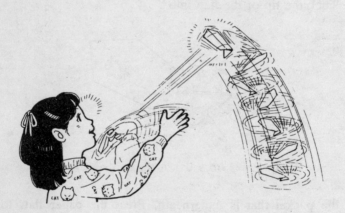

Mini Aeroplane

A while ago, when we were working in southern Germany, the son of the family we were staying with showed us how to make two quick and easy aeroplanes. This is one of them.

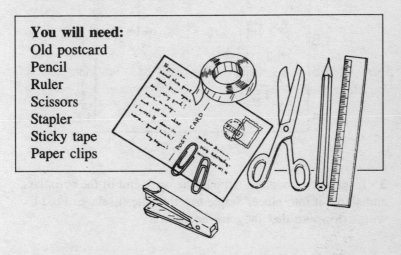

You will need:
Old postcard
Pencil
Ruler
Scissors
Stapler
Sticky tape
Paper clips

1 Place the postcard on a flat surface, lengthways on. Fold it in half from bottom to top.

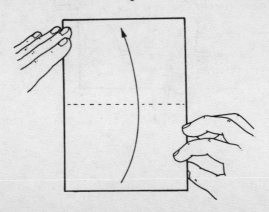

2 Using the pencil and ruler, mark and measure out the aeroplane and its tail, as shown, on to the postcard. Carefully cut along your pencil lines. Discard the shaded parts and one tail.

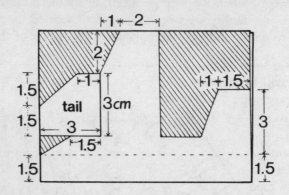

3 Insert the remaining tail into the back end of the aeroplane and staple it into place. Staple together the fuselage. Fold the wings down so that they are horizontal.

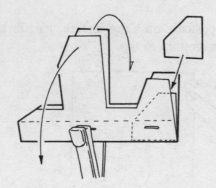

4 Hold together the wings with a piece of sticky tape. Fasten a paper clip on to the aeroplane's nose.

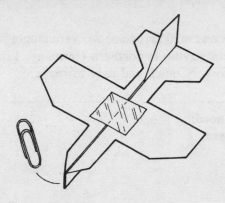

5 Throw the aeroplane in a gentle glide. If it suddenly nosedives, place a paper clip inside the fuselage. Keep on adjusting the nose weight until you are satisfied with the aeroplane's glide.

King Wing

This is the second mini aeroplane we were taught how to make when we were staying in southern Germany. Like the other one, it is also very quick and easy to make.

You will need:
Old Postcard
Pencil
Ruler
Scissors
Stapler
Sticky tape
Paper clips

1 Repeat step 1 of the MINI AEROPLANE on page 91. Using the pencil and ruler, mark and measure out the aeroplane and its tail, as shown, on to the postcard. Carefully cut along your pencil lines. Discard the shaded parts and one tail.

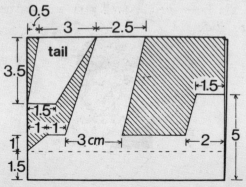

2 Insert the remaining tail into the back end of the aeroplane and staple it into place. Staple together the fuselage. Fold the wings down so that they are horizontal.

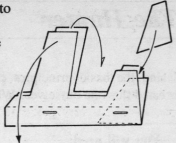

3 Hold together the wings with a piece of sticky tape. Fasten a paper clip on to the aeroplane's nose. Curve the wings gently upwards.

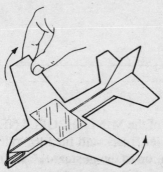

4 Throw the aeroplane in a gentle glide. If it suddenly nosedives, place a paper clip inside the fuselage. Keep on adjusting the nose weight until you are satisfied with the aeroplane's glide.

The Hunter

Using the basic principles of the previous aeroplanes, we created this one ourselves. Why not try and create your own?

You will need:
Old postcard
Pencil
Ruler
Scissors
Stapler
Sticky tape
Paper clips

---

1 Repeat step 1 of the MINI AEROPLANE on page 91. Using the pencil and ruler, mark and measure out the aeroplane and its tail, as shown, on to the postcard. Carefully cut along your pencil lines. Discard the shaded parts and one tail.

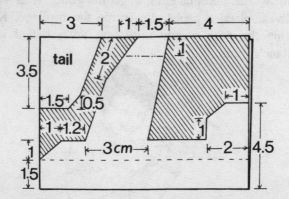

2 Insert the remaining tail into the back end of the aeroplane and staple it into place. Staple together the fuselage. Fold the wings down so that they are horizontal.

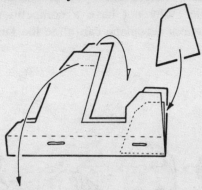

3 Hold together the wings with a piece of sticky tape. Fasten a paper clip on to the aeroplane's nose.

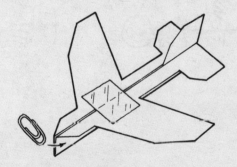

4 Fold the tips of each wing up. This fold should start about 1cm from the wing tip.

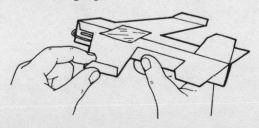

5 Throw the aeroplane in a gentle glide. If it suddenly nosedives, place a paper clip inside the fuselage. Keep on adjusting the nose weight until you are satisfied with the aeroplane's glide. Why not have a competition with your friends to see whose aeroplane can glide the farthest?

Straw Aeroplane

The straw aeroplane is a long-range glider. With its large wings and weighty nose it should cruise a long way.

You will need:
Scissors
Sheet of strong paper (typing paper is ideal)
Pencil
Ruler
Glue
Piece of tin foil
Drinking straw

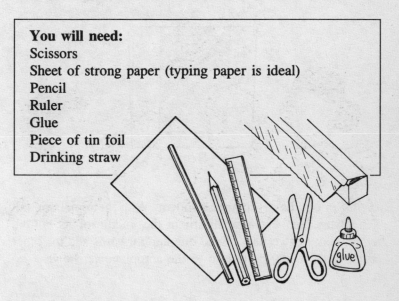

1 Cut two strips of paper, one measuring 5cm × 10cm and the other 2.5cm × 9cm.

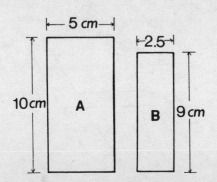

2 Place strip A on a flat surface, lengthways on. Fold it in half from bottom to top. Using the pencil and ruler, mark and measure out the aeroplane and its tail, as shown, on to strip A. Carefully cut along your pencil lines. Discard the shaded part and one tail.

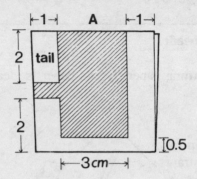

3 Open out the aeroplane as shown. With the remaining tail lengthways on, cut a small slit in the middle of its bottom edge, making two flaps. Bend one flap forwards and the other backwards. Glue the tail on to the aeroplane as shown.

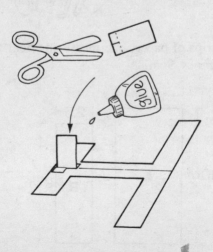

4 Place strip B on a flat surface, sideways on. Using the pencil and ruler, mark and measure out strip B as shown. Fold its bottom edge over to meet the pencil line that is 0.5cm down from the top edge.

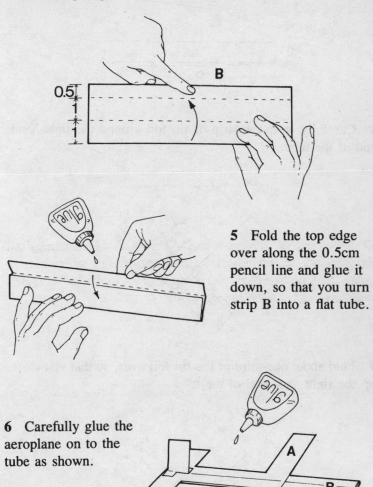

5 Fold the top edge over along the 0.5cm pencil line and glue it down, so that you turn strip B into a flat tube.

6 Carefully glue the aeroplane on to the tube as shown.

7 Cut a strip of tin foil measuring 1cm × 9cm.

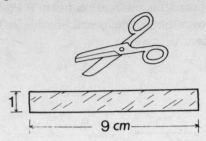

8 Carefully wrap the strip of tin foil around the right-hand end of the tube.

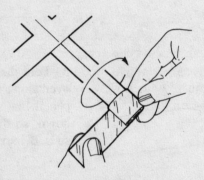

9 Fold about one-third of the tin foil over, so that you close up the right-hand end of the tube.

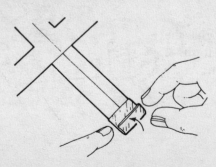

10 Carefully insert the drinking straw into the tube from the left-hand end. Be careful NOT to push the straw through the tube or out through the opposite end. Curve the aeroplane's wings gently upwards.

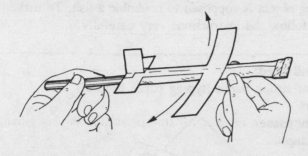

11 Place the drinking straw to your lips with the aeroplane pointing UPWARDS. Blow into the straw to make the aeroplane shoot off and glide into the air. If the aeroplane suddenly nosedives, either add on a little tin foil or take some off. Keep on adjusting the nose weight until you are satisfied with the aeroplane's glide.

Flying Skate

This flying object is supposed to resemble a fish. To make it fly well, follow the instructions very carefully.

You will need:
Sheet of strong paper (typing paper is ideal)
Scissors
A paper tissue
Sticky tape

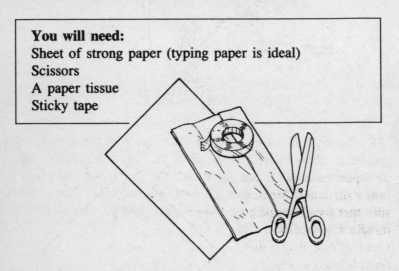

1 Place the sheet of paper on a flat surface, sideways on. Fold the left-hand side over to lie along the top edge, to make a triangle.

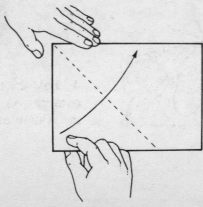

2 Cut along the right-hand side edge of the triangle, and discard the rectangular shape of paper.

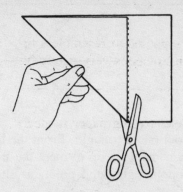

3 Open the triangle out into a diamond. Making sure that the diamond's middle fold-line is vertical, fold it in half from bottom to top.

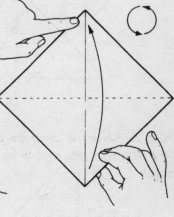

4 Fold the two top corners over to meet the bottom edge.

5 Fold the top edge over to meet the bottom edge. Press the paper flat.

6 Open the paper out into a triangle. From the bottom edge cut a slit in the paper that goes up to meet the farthest fold-line. Cut off the bottom right-hand point, as shown by the shading.

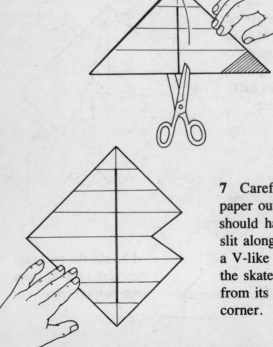

7 Carefully open the paper out. The paper should have a vertical slit along its middle and a V-like shape (which is the skate's tail) cut out from its right-hand corner.

8 Turn the paper around so that the slit is horizontal and the skate's tail is at the top. Fold the bottom corner over to meet the slit.

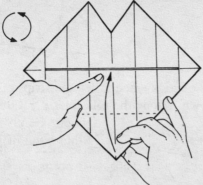

9 Fold the bottom edge over to meet the slit.

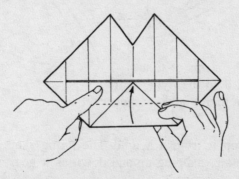

10 For the last time fold the bottom edge over to meet the slit, to make a thin band of paper.

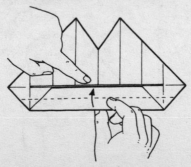

11 Cut two long strips of tissue each about 1cm wide.

12 With pieces of sticky tape fasten the strips of tissue on to the paper as shown. Along the fold-lines pleat the skate's tail section. Gently curve the thin band of paper.

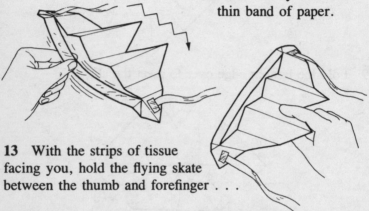

13 With the strips of tissue facing you, hold the flying skate between the thumb and forefinger . . .

14 and drop it from a height. The flying skate will glide through the air, flapping up and down as it goes.

Kite Aeroplane

Megumi learned how to make this flying object during her childhood days in Japan.

You will need:
A 16cm square of strong paper (typing paper is
    ideal)
Scissors
A paper tissue
Sticky tape

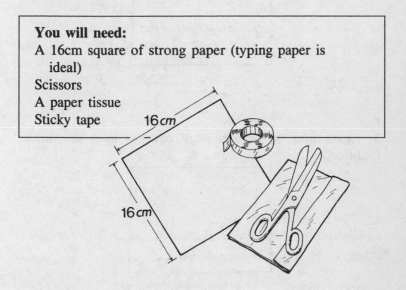

16 cm

16 cm

1 Place the square of paper on a flat surface. Fold and unfold it in half from bottom to top.

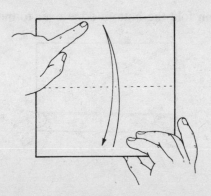

2 Fold the bottom edge over to meet the middle fold-line.

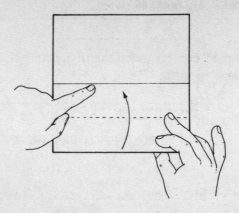

3 Again fold the bottom edge over to meet the middle fold-line.

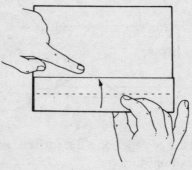

4 Once again fold the bottom edge over to meet the middle fold-line.

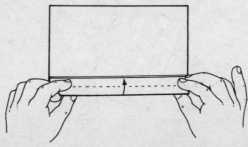

5 Last of all fold the bottom edge over along the middle fold line, to make a thin band of paper.

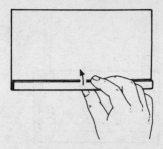

6 Fold the left and right-hand sides over a little.

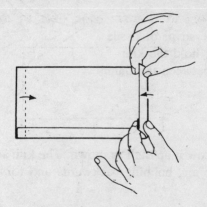

7 Cut two long strips of tissue each about 1cm wide.

8 With pieces of sticky tape fasten the strips of tissue on to the paper as shown. Gently curve the paper to finish off the kite aeroplane.

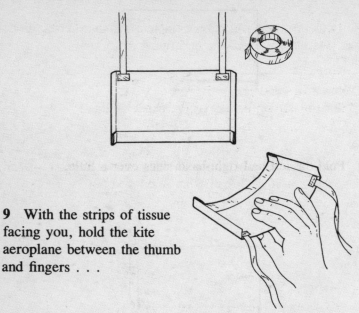

9 With the strips of tissue facing you, hold the kite aeroplane between the thumb and fingers . . .

10 and throw it up high as shown. The kite aeroplane will fly through the air, bobbing backwards and forward as it goes.

Traditional Dart

No book on flying objects is complete without the traditional dart. Do have fun making and flying it.

You will need:
Sheet of strong paper (typing paper is ideal)

---

1 Place the sheet of paper on a flat surface, sideways on. Fold and unfold it in half from bottom to top.

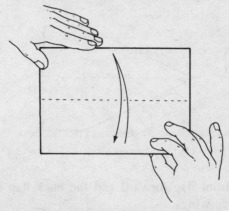

2 Fold the top and bottom left-hand corners over to meet the middle fold-line.

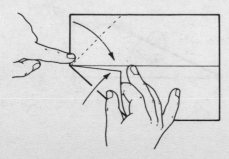

3 From the left-hand point fold the sloping edges over to meet the middle fold-line.

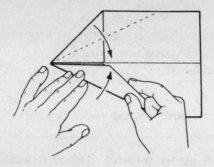

4 Turn the paper over from top to bottom. Fold it in half from bottom to top.

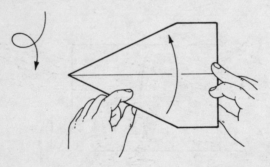

5 Fold the front flap forward and the back flap behind, to make the dart's wings.

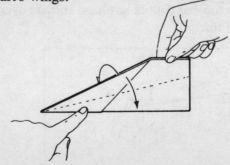

6 Lift the wings up so that they are horizontal. Hold the dart between the thumb and forefinger . . .

7 and throw it gently forward. Try to increase the dart's thrust by throwing it harder. Always be very careful NOT to hit anyone, especially in their eyes, when you are throwing your dart.

Origami Aeroplane

With a few, quick folds you can make a very effective aeroplane. We hope that you have a lot of fun flying it.

You will need:
Sheet of strong paper (typing paper is ideal)

1 Place the sheet of paper on a flat surface, sideways on. Fold and unfold it in half from bottom to top.

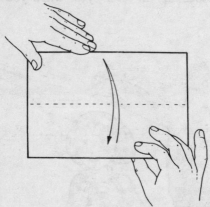

2 Fold the top and bottom left-hand corners over to meet the middle fold-line.

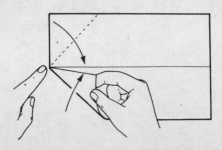

3 Fold the left-hand point over towards the right as shown.

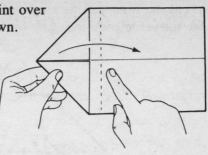

4 Again fold the top and bottom left-hand corners over to meet the middle fold-line.

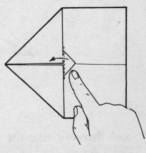

5 Fold the protruding triangle over towards the left as shown.

6 Turn the paper over from top to bottom. Fold it in half from bottom to top.

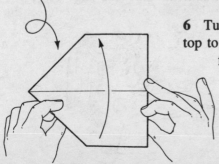

7 Fold the front flap forward and the back flap behind, to make the aeroplane's wings.

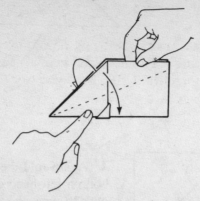

8 Lift the wings up so that they are horizontal. Hold the origami aeroplane between the thumb and forefinger . . .

9 and throw it like the traditional dart (see page 113).

Swallow Aeroplane

This is probably one of the best flying objects ever created. Steve learnt how to make this aeroplane from his grandfather, and he has never forgotten it. We hope you won't either.

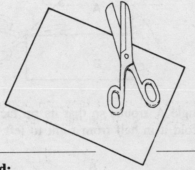

You will need:
Sheet of strong paper (typing paper is ideal)
Scissors

1 Place the sheet of paper on a flat surface, lengthways on. Fold the top edge over to lie along the left-hand side, so that you make a triangle.

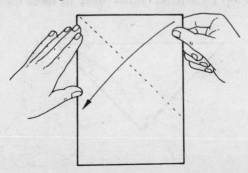

2 Cut along the bottom edge of the triangle, to make traingle A and rectangle B. Place rectangle B to one side, later on it will be used in the making of the tail.

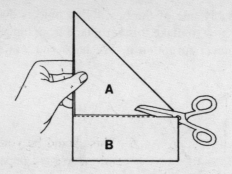

3 Turn triangle A around so that its tip faces towards you. Fold and unfold it in half from right to left.

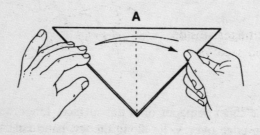

4 Fold the top right-hand corner over to meet the bottom point.

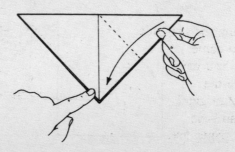

5 Turn the paper over and repeat step 4.

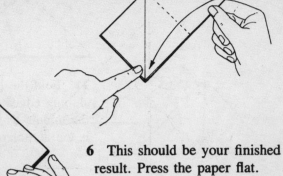

6 This should be your finished result. Press the paper flat.

7 Put your fingers inside the paper and separate . . .

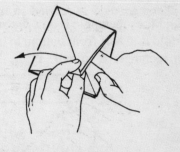

8 the front from the back, so . . .

9 allowing the two side corners to come together. You have now made the traditional origami waterbomb base. Press the paper flat.

10 Fold the top two bottom corners over to meet the top.

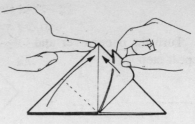

11 Fold the lower two sloping edges over to meet the middle as shown. This is the aeroplane's body.

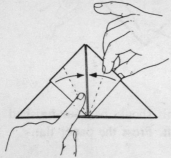

12 Place rectangle B on a flat surface, sideways on. Fold and unfold it in half from bottom to top. Along the middle fold-line cut rectangle B in half. Place the top half to one side.

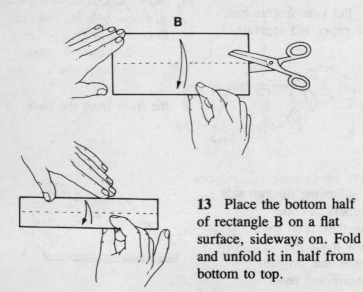

13 Place the bottom half of rectangle B on a flat surface, sideways on. Fold and unfold it in half from bottom to top.

122

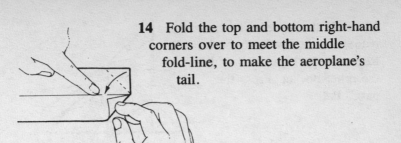

14 Fold the top and bottom right-hand corners over to meet the middle fold-line, to make the aeroplane's tail.

15 Insert the tail deep into the body as shown.

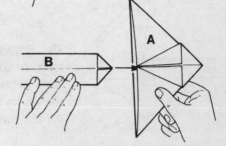

16 Turn the tail and body over from top to bottom. Fold the right-hand point over as far as shown, to make two top pockets.

17 Insert your finger inside one of the pockets. Pull the pocket . . .

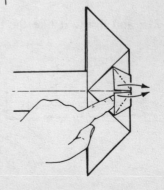

18 over to the right, so making it look like a swallow's beak. Repeat steps 17 and 18 with the other pocket. Press the paper flat.

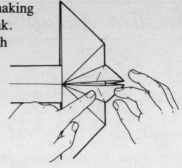

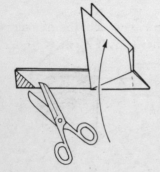

19 Fold the tail and body in half from bottom to top. Cut off the tail's bottom left-hand point as shown by the shading, to finish off the swallow aeroplane.

20 Open out the swallow aeroplane so that its wings slightly point upwards. Hold the aeroplane between the thumb and forefinger . . .

21 and throw it like the traditional dart (see page 113).

Swallow Aeroplane Aerobatics

Once you have mastered the skill of flying the swallow aeroplane, try these aerobatics.

Steady Glide

● Hold the swallow aeroplane between the thumb and forefinger and with a gentle throw launch it out of your hand.

The Swoop

● Hold the swallow aeroplane between the thumb and forefinger and with a medium-to-hard throw launch it straight ahead.

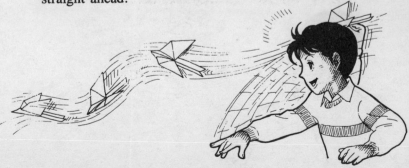

The Loop

- Hold the swallow aeroplane between the thumb and forefinger and with a HARD throw launch it straight ahead.

Tail Toss

- Hold the swallow aeroplane as shown and throw it tail first as if it were a ball. The swallow aeroplane will flick around as it leaves your hand. The tail toss needs a bit of practice. But it is worth it because the result is higher and longer flights.

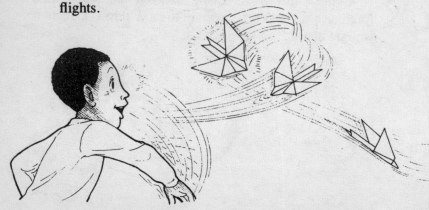

Flick Roll

● Hold the swallow aeroplane by one wing and throw it as if it were a frisbee. You will be surprised at what happens.

We do hope you have had
a lot of fun and enjoyment with
AMAZING FLYING OBJECTS.